Ordering Information:
Special discounts are available on quantity purchases by corporations, associations, and others. For details, contact the Author at www.yehudaremer.com.

This is a work of fiction. Names, characters, businesses, places, events and incidents are either the products of the author's imagination or used in a fictitious manner. Any resemblance to actual persons, living or dead, or actual events is purely coincidental.

Printed in the United States of America

Illustrated by AmmarDegas

A wise man's mind tends to his right,
while a fool's mind tends to his left.
Even on the road as the fool walks,
he lacks sense,
and proclaims to all that he is a fool.

Ecclesiastes 10:2-3

10 LiTTLe LibeRaLs

standing in a line.

WE ACCEPT
FOOD
STAMPS
EBT
CARDS

TOLD TO GET A REAL JOB...

don't believe in Heaven.

Got a little blessing...

7 Little Liberals

wanna become chicks.

6 Little Liberals

tRieD veRY HARd to tHRive.

NOW tHEY'RE oNLY FivE.

5 Little LibeRaLs

Rioting at a store.

4 Little Liberals

believe that they are free.

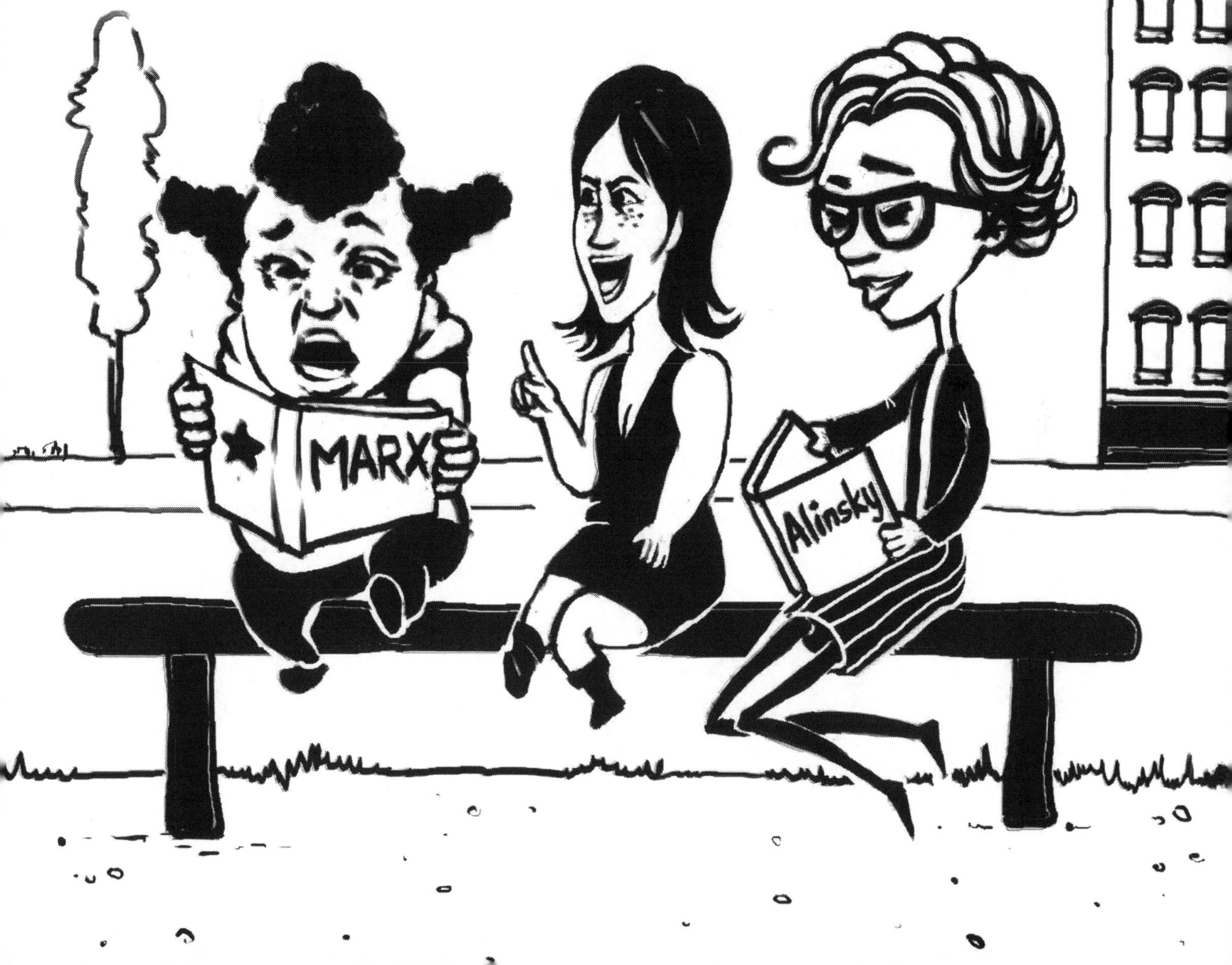

3 LitrLe LiBERALs

tRied to pull a coup.

met by navy SEALs...

2 LittLe LibERALs

aRGueD about an aboRtion...

CRYiNG iT's aLL NoT FaiR.

NO MORE LITTLE LIBERALS

tHEY ALL JUST FLEW away.

and God bless the usa.

Made in the USA
Lexington, KY
01 December 2017